**Principles of
Two-Dimensional
Form**

14.95

wucius wong   **Principles of Two-Dimensional Form**

VNR | VAN NOSTRAND REINHOLD COMPANY
New York

Copyright © 1988 by Van Nostrand Reinhold
Company Inc.
Library of Congress Catalog Card Number 87-8150
ISBN 0-442-29180-9

Printed in the United States of America
Designed by Wucius Wong

Van Nostrand Reinhold Company Inc.
115 Fifth Avenue
New York, New York 10003

Van Nostrand Reinhold Company Limited
Molly Millars Lane
Wokingham, Berkshire RG11 2PY, England

Van Nostrand Reinhold
480 La Trobe Street
Melbourne, Victoria 3000, Australia

Macmillan of Canada
Division of Canada Publishing Corporation
164 Commander Boulevard
Agincourt, Ontario M1S 3C7, Canada

16 15 14 13 12 11 10 9 8 7 6 5 4 3 2 1

**Library of Congress Cataloging-in-Publication
Data**

Wong, Wucius.
   Principles of two-dimensional form.
   Includes index.
   1. Design.   2. Visual perception.   I. Title.
NK1505.W6   1987   745.4   87-8150
ISBN 0-442-29180-9 (pbk.)

CONTENTS

PREFACE

This book provides a general investigation into the different possibilities for creating two-dimensional forms. It examines the various types of forms as well as the methods of developing and manipulating them. Special emphasis is given to representational forms (overlooked in most books on two-dimensional design).

This book can be considered a sequel to my earlier book *Principles of Two-Dimensional Design,* or as a totally new approach to the subject. This text treats form, on the one hand, as the fundamental aspect of design (it is often the starting point for experiments in a basic design course). On the other hand, form is the ultimate concern of the professional designer, who sees design as part of the process for achieving a form that communicates to the viewer.

This book will serve not only as an essential aid for students, but also as a reference tool for the graphic designer. Numerous illustrations are featured.

Most of the illustrations were provided by the Swire School of Design of the Hong Kong Polytechnic and the Hong Kong Institute of Visual Studies. I wish to thank Mr. Michael Farr, head of the Swire School of Design, and Mr. Hon Bing-wah, director of the Hong Kong Institute of Visual Studies, for permission to reproduce their students' work. I am indebted to Mr. Leung Kui-ting, who has taught in both institutions, introducing exercises in representational forms that are important to the conception of a part of this book.

For preparation of the text, diagrams, and photographic prints as well as the overall layout of the book, I have relied on my wife, Pansy, whose experience in publication design has made her my collaborator. Her contribution here deserves greater recognition than any indication of gratitude.

This book would not have been possible without the students' high-quality illustrations. I am grateful to all of them.

PART I
ASPECTS OF FORM

Broadly speaking, all that is visible has form. Form is everything that can be seen—everything with shape, size, color, and texture that occupies space, marks position, and indicates direction. A created form can be based on reality—recognizable—or abstract—unrecognizable. A form might be created to convey a meaning or message, or it could be merely decorative. It might be simple or complex, harmonious or discordant.

In a narrow sense, forms are self-contained, positive shapes that occupy space and are distinguishable from a background.

Because we live in three-dimensional space, our experience of form is primarily three-dimensional. A three-dimensional form is one that we can walk toward, away from, or around; it can be viewed from different angles and distances. If it is within reach, we might touch or even handle it.

A three-dimensional form is not necessarily stationary. A living creature can be described as a three-dimensional form that runs, flies, swims, or moves part of its body. A man-made three-dimensional form can consist of moving, movable, or modular elements. Three-dimensional forms interact with other three-dimensional forms in the environment.

Man's writings, drawings, paintings, decorations, designs, and doodles are of shapes and colors that can be perceived as two-dimensional forms.

Natural surfaces that display textures and patterns are also sometimes perceived as two-dimensional forms. We can, however, regard two-dimensional forms essentially as a human creation for the communication of ideas, the recording of experiences, the expression of feelings and emotions, the decoration of plain surfaces, or the conveyance of artistic visions.

Two-dimensional forms consist of points, lines, and/or planes on a flat surface.

Our visual experiences of the three-dimensional world influence our perception of two-dimensional forms. A shape against an empty background appears to be surrounded by a void. Volume and thickness can be added to a shape, which can be rotated in space to exhibit different views.

The terms *shape* and *form* are often used synonymously, but their meanings are not the same. A shape is an area easily defined with an outline. A shape that is given volume and thickness and that can exhibit different views becomes a form. Forms display some depth and volume—characteristics associated with three-dimensional figures, whereas shapes are forms depicted at particular angles, from particular distances. A form can therefore have many shapes.

Figures 1 through 4 show the same leaf form in a variety of shapes.

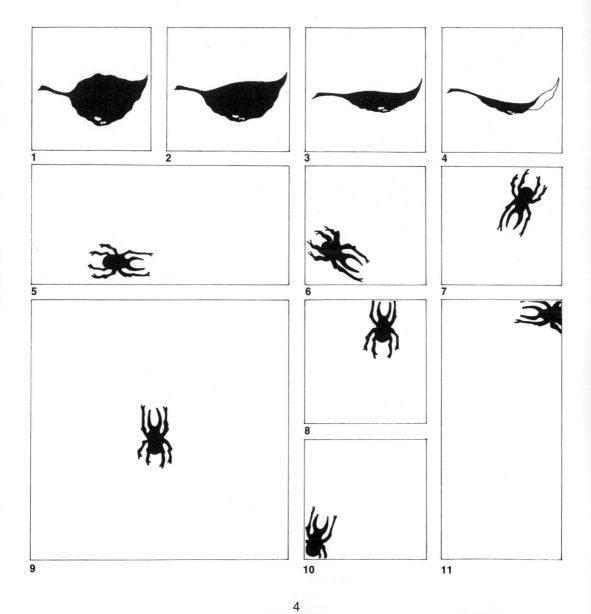

4

A design normally begins as an area that is bound by four edges at right angles to one another. These edges constitute the *frame of reference,* which has a shape of its own.

Within the frame of reference, a form or numerous forms can be introduced. A *figure-ground* situation thus emerges; forms are seen as *figures,* and the space behind forms and the space between them and the frame of reference as *ground* or *background* in the resulting *composition.* A composition is the visual effect that is generated by the interaction of figures and ground.

Furthermore, the frame of reference provides scale—we get a sense of the *size* of forms—and establishes the *positions* and *directions* of elements.

Figures 5 through 11 feature the same form (and the same shape) in different compositions. Notice how different compositions result from different frames of reference (figs. 5–8); how compositions look smaller when the frame of reference is large (fig. 9) and how it can be cropped by the frame of reference when the form moves partially beyond its boundary (figs. 10, 11).

Form is *positive space,* space that is occupied. Unoccupied space surrounding a form is known as *negative space.* Positive space is seen as a positive shape (fig. 12). When negative space is surrounded with positive shapes, it becomes a negative shape (fig. 13).

A shape is perceived as a flat form when it shows no thickness, fully faces the viewer, and suggests no depth. This is the effect created by pasting a shape cut from thin paper on another piece of paper. When one shape overlaps another, some depth is created (fig. 14). When the same shape is shown curled, folded, or flipped, a form of considerable depth is introduced (figs. 15–17). The same shape can be displayed at different sizes in the same composition; a sequence of receding forms suggests infinite depth (fig. 18).

A shape that is given thickness or volume transforms a flat, two-dimensional space within the frame of reference into space of appropriate depth (fig. 19). Flat and voluminous forms, shallow and deep spaces, produce different visual illusions, which must be considered when creating two-dimensional designs.

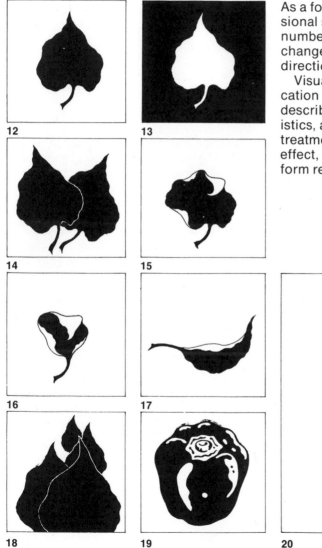

As a form takes shape on a two-dimensional surface, it can be depicted in a number of different ways without a change in its size, color, position, or direction.

Visualizing a form requires the application of points, lines, and planes that describe its contours, surface characteristics, and other details. Each method of treatment results in a different visual effect, although the general shape of the form remains the same.

12

13

14

15

16

17

18

19

20

Visualization with Lines

Visualization with Planes

A line is created by moving an appropriate tool across a surface by hand. It is easy to visualize a form constructed with lines. It is somewhat like drawing, except that solid lines of uniform breadth might be used in design creation.

An outline is the most economical expression of basic visual information (fig. 20). If a fine line does not achieve the visual impact desired, a much bolder line could replace it (fig. 21).

Within the outline details can be introduced that provide descriptive information and strengthen the connections and divisions of elements, the apparent volume and depth, and the spatial sequence from foreground to background of the form (fig. 22).

A form can also be visualized with primary and secondary lines to clarify its structure; in this case, lines of two or more uniform breadths may be used (fig. 23).

The shape outlined in figure 20 can be painted black to create a continuous flat plane. The result is a silhouette—the simplest expression of a form (fig. 24).

Black and white areas can be easily reversed; a black shape on a white background becomes a white, or negative, shape on a black background (fig. 25).

A shape that is achieved with one continuous plane is usually void of details. Negative lines (white lines on the solid black plane) can be used to introduce details. Negative lines separate a large plane into smaller planes (fig. 26).

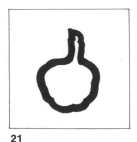

21

22

23

24

Lines are used to create seemingly light shapes, whereas planes create heavy shapes. Lines and planes used together allow light and heavy areas to coexist within a shape; details can be introduced where necessary. This manner of visualization is particularly suitable for adding light and shade to enhance the effect of volume in a form (fig. 27).

25

26

27

Visualization with Points

Visualization with Texture

Repeated points can be arranged to outline a form (fig. 28). Points can also be grouped as a plane to suggest a form (fig. 29). When used to create planes, points produce texture.

Texture can be created with points, short lines, long lines, or any combination of these. Texture can be shown as a regular pattern, or as an irregular pattern, with slight variations in the shape or size of similar elements (figs. 30, 31).

Texture generally adds visual variations to planes and surface characteristics to forms. Texture can also be applied in light dark modulations to establish volume (fig. 32).

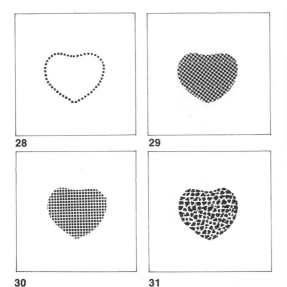

28

29

30

31

32

Forms can be broadly classified according to their particular contents.

A form that contains a recognizable *subject* communicates with viewers in more than purely visual terms. This is called a *representational* form. When a form does not contain a recognizable subject, it is considered *nonrepresentational* or abstract.

A representational form can be rendered with photographic realism or with some degree of abstraction—as long as it is not so abstract as to make the subject unrecognizable (fig. 33). If the subject cannot be identified, the form is nonrepresentational.

Sometimes the subject of a representational form is fantastic. The form, however, will present a transformed reality, one that suggests volume and space, so the fantastic subject conveys a kind of reality to the viewer (fig. 34).

33

34

Natural Forms

Man-made Forms

Representational forms can be further classified according to subject matter. If the subject is something found in nature, the form can be described as a *natural* form (fig. 35).

Natural forms include living organisms and inanimate objects that exist on the earth's surface, in the oceans, or in the sky.

Man-made forms are representational forms that are derived from objects and environments created by man (fig. 36). They can feature buildings, furniture, vehicles, machines, tools, household products, toys, apparel, or stationery, to name a few possibilities.

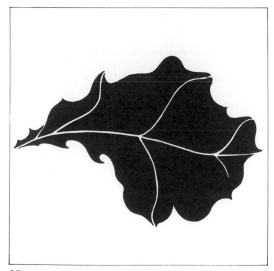

35

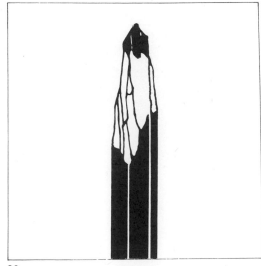

36

Verbal Forms

Abstract Forms

Written language consists of characters, letters, words, and numerals that make precise visual communication possible. A form based on an element of written language is a a *verbal* form (fig. 37).

A verbal form is representational in that it depicts a recognizable idea, rather than something that exists in a material sense.

An abstract form lacks a recognizable subject (fig. 38). It could be the designer's intention to create a form that represents nothing. This form could have been based on a subject that has become obliterated after excessive transformation, or it could have been the result of experimentation with materials that led to unexpected results.

An abstract form expresses a designer's sensitivity to shape, color, and composition without relying on recognizable elements.

37

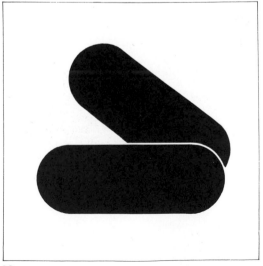

38

The same form, whether representational or abstract, can be expressed in different shapes. This does not mean that it must be seen from different views, angles, and distances, or that it must be moved or transformed; the different *approaches* possible in visual creation produce different results.

One approach is to draw the shape freehand in a somewhat *calligraphic* manner. Another approach is to create an *organic* shape by reducing a shape to all smooth curves. A third approach is to use only straight lines, circles, or arcs to establish a *geometric* shape.

The movement of the hand, the drawing tool, the medium, and the drawing surface are apparent in a calligraphic shape. The tool is generally a pen, pencil, or brush, whose particular characteristics are apparent in the finished form (fig. 39).

39

Organic Shapes

Geometric Shapes

An organic shape displays convexities and concavities with softly flowing curves. It also includes points of contact between curves (fig. 40).

When visualizing a form as an organic shape, all pen lines and brushstrokes should be controlled to minimize traces of hand movements, and the recognizable effects of particular tools.

A geometric shape relies on mechanical means of construction. Straight lines have to be drawn with rulers, circles and arcs with compasses. Sharpness and precision must prevail. All traces of hand movements or tools should be eliminated as much as possible (fig. 41).

40

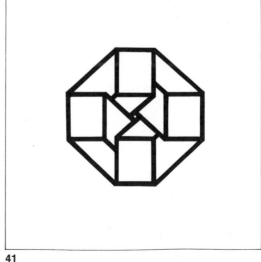

41

PART II
DESIGNING A FORM

Design is the entire composition of which form is the most conspicuous part. Sometimes all visual elements in a design are collectively referred to as form, but it is more common that clearly defined shapes are taken as forms, which constitute the composition.

Designing a form can be a process separate from designing a composition, although one affects the other considerably. It is often useful to see a form first in isolation and then as an element among other elements. A designer should explore extensively the numerous options for shaping a form.

If a composition consists of only one form, it is called a *singular* form.   A composition with a singular form does not have a conglomerate of smaller, clearly distinguishable forms (fig. 42).

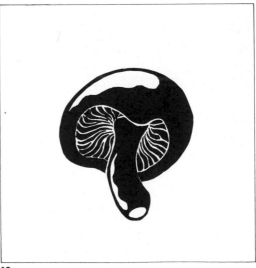

42

Plural Forms

When a form is repeated in a composition, it is called a *plural* form.

The *components* of a plural form might vary slightly, but must be closely associated, overlapped, interlocked, or joined in order for them to be read as one image in the composition (fig. 43).

Compound Forms

Different forms can be united to create a *compound* form (fig. 44).

A plural can become a compound form by adding an element that is different in form.

43

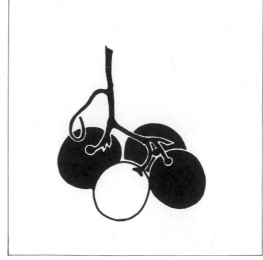

44

Unit Forms

Superunit Forms

A form used repeatedly in a composition is a *unit* form (fig. 45).

Unlike the components of a plural form, unit forms are individual elements that do not constitute a larger form. Unit forms are often used in patternlike designs.

Two or more unit forms can be grouped together and then repeated in a design. Each group is considered a *superunit* form (fig. 46).

A superunit form is different from a plural form in that the elements of a plural form combine to produce a single shape; a superunit form can be a loosely packed group of unit forms.

45

46

Forms can be designed either as geometric or as organic shapes. Generally speaking, natural forms are more easily adapted to organic shapes, whereas man-made and abstract forms are more easily expressed as geometric shapes.

Geometric shapes are created using straight lines and circles. The nature of geometry demands careful planning in order for lines to meet at a certain angle, for one arc to flow into another, to divide space equally, and to establish a regular pattern.

A straight line is the shortest distance between two points.

A straight line with breadth displays weight in addition to length and direction (fig. 47).

As a line becomes heavier, its endings become more and more prominent, displaying shape characteristics of their own (figs. 48, 49).

Used as an edge to a plane, a line divides positive and negative space or distinguishes one plane from another (fig 50).

47

48

49

50

Circles

A circle is established with a fixed center and radius. Only its circumference is visible after the circle is drawn.

Described as a linear shape, the circle is an unbroken line that encloses space. This unbroken line can also acquire breadth (figs. 51, 52). It separates the space it surrounds from the space surrounding it.

As a planar shape, the circle displays a maximum area within a minimum boundary without angularity or direction (fig. 53).

A fragment of a circle, part of its circumference, forms an arc (fig. 54).

An isolated arc is visualized as a linear shape of definite breadth, whose endings might be shaped (figs. 55–57).

51

52

54

55

53

56

57

Relating Straight Lines

Two straight lines can be brought together in numerous ways by changing their positions and/or directions. Two lines can touch, join, or overlap (figs. 58–61). Lines can be joined end to end or end to edge (figs. 59, 62). Bold lines with curved endings require special treatment (figs. 63–66).

Bold lines can overlap, forming a negative shape in the overlapped area (fig. 67).

Parallel bold lines can touch or join without creating one continuous line (figs. 68, 69).

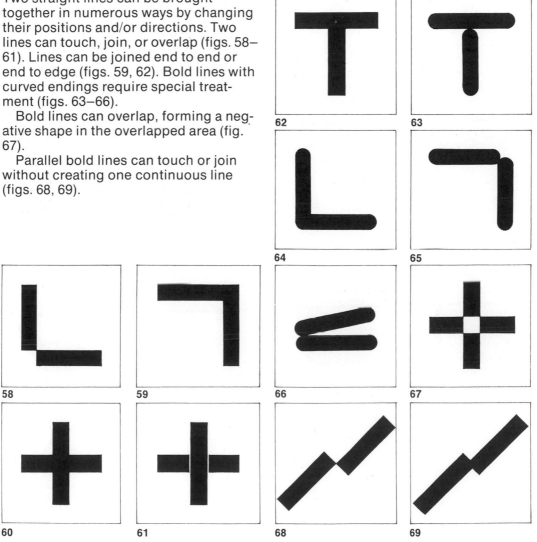

62

63

64

65

58

59

66

67

60

61

68

69

Relating Circles

Circles can touch, join, overlap, or inter-lock (figs. 70–73). Boldly drawn circum-ferences can lead to more variations (figs. 74–79).

Circles of different sizes can be super-imposed, with larger ones containing smaller ones (figs. 80, 81).

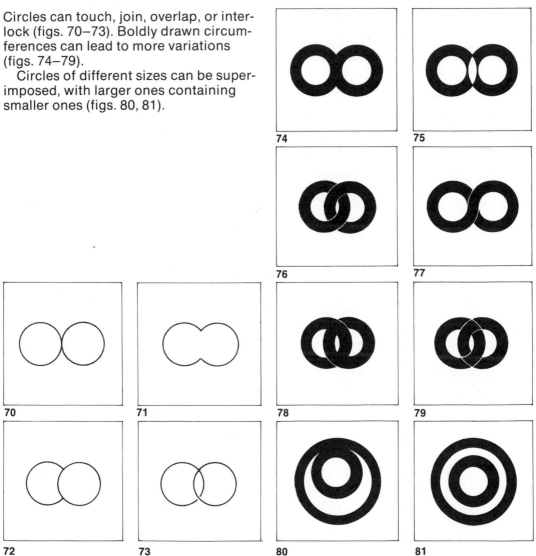

70

71

72

73

74

75

76

77

78

79

80

81

Relating Arcs

Two arcs can touch, join, overlap, or interlock (figs. 82–86). Arcs that are joined can produce an enclosed space or a winding curve (figs. 87, 88). The end of arcs can vary to achieve different effects (figs. 89, 90). Arcs of different sizes can be arranged with or without connecting their endings (figs. 91, 92).

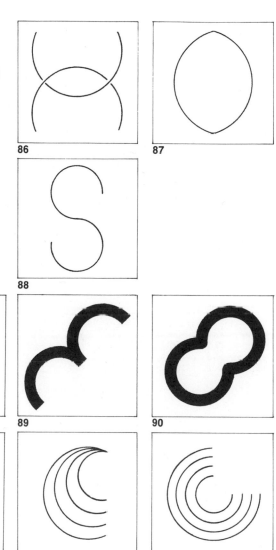

86

87

88

82

83

89

90

84

85

91

92

Relating Straight Lines, Circles, and Arcs

Straight lines, circles, and arcs can be made to relate in a multitude of ways by manipulating their breadths, their endings, their ending-to-ending joints (figs. 93, 94), their ending-to-edge joints (fig. 95), their edge-to-edge joints (fig. 96), the way they overlap (fig. 97), the way they interlock (fig. 98), the way they interpenetrate (fig. 99), the way they interweave (fig. 100), their continuities (figs. 101, 102), and their enclosures (figs. 103, 104).

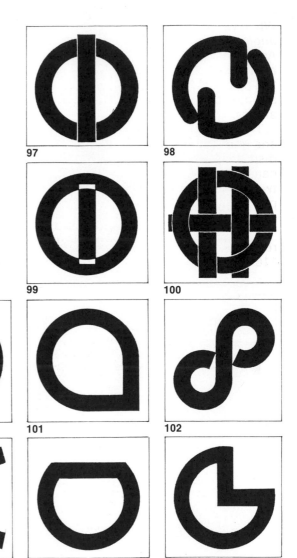

97

98

99

100

93

94

101

102

95

96

103

104

Angles and Pointed Tips

When two lines meet, they form an *angle.* Angles are measured in degrees. Angles of 30, 45, 60, 90, and 120 degrees are considered regular angles. Figures 105 through 109 show shapes constructed of straight lines at regular angles.

The endings of two arcs, or of one arc and one straight line, can also be joined, displaying a pointed tip. Just as angles can be acute or obtuse, the place where two lines meet to form an angle (the pointed tip) can be sharp or blunt (figs. 110–14).

Angles and tips in a shape can be rounded by using tiny arcs (figs. 115, 116).

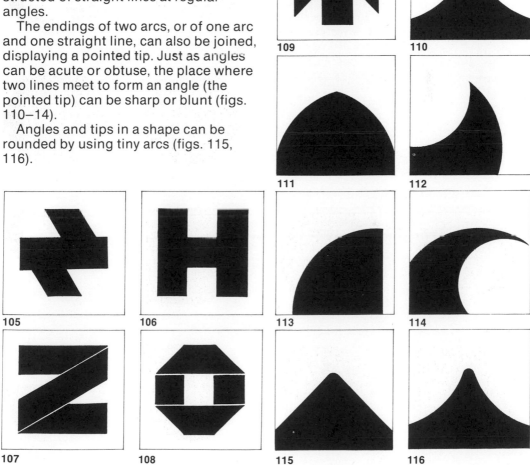

109

110

111

112

105

106

113

114

107

108

115

116

The Addition of Planes

The space enclosed by lines can be filled with solid color to form a plane. Two planes can be combined, or added, whether or not they are of the same shape or size (figs. 117–120).

Planes might overlap or intersect with other planes, while the shape of an individual plane maintains its separate identity (figs. 121–24). Shapes thus created are less seen as singular forms, but more as plural or compound forms (see page 17).

Two planes that have been combined might have some common edges, which result in a shape without easily discernible components (figs. 125, 126).

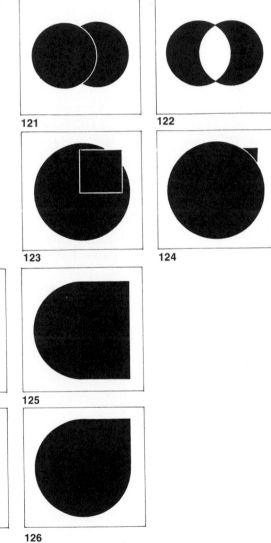

121

122

123

124

117

118

125

119

120

126

The Subtraction of Planes

The Interpenetration of Planes

When a negative plane overlaps a positive plane, space appears to have been subtracted from the positive plane. The resulting shape shows a missing portion where the negative plane merges with the background (figs. 127, 128). Sometimes subtraction leads to loose parts (fig. 129).

A smaller negative plane can be completely contained within a larger positive plane (fig. 130).

Two planes can create a transparent effect by forming a negative shape within an overlapped area (figs. 131, 132). Negative shapes might become positive when overlapped within a design that includes the interpenetration of more than two planes (fig. 133).

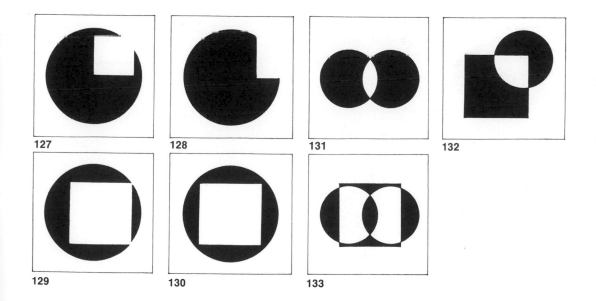

127

128

131

132

129

130

133

27

The Multiplication of Planes

The same plane can be *multiplied,* or used repeatedly without change in shape or size. Each plane is thus seen as a component of a plural form.

A plane that is multiplied can produce separate planes (fig. 134), planes that touch (fig. 135), planes that are joined (fig. 136), planes that overlap (figs. 137, 138), planes that interpenetrate (fig. 139), planes that combine positive and negative shapes (fig. 140).

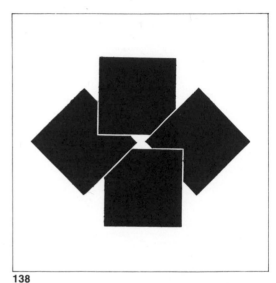

138

134

135

139

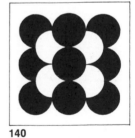

140

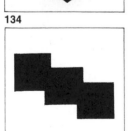

136

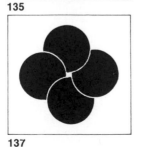

137

A plane can be divided into equal or unequal parts. Negative lines can be introduced with gaps between dissected shapes (figs. 141, 142). The slight displacement of dissected shapes can lead to interesting effects, but the original shape of the plane must remain recognizable (fig. 143).

Dissected shapes can touch, join, overlap, or interpenetrate (fig. 144).

143

141

142

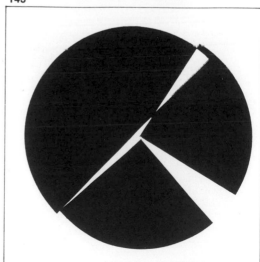

144

Varying the Size of Planes

A plane can be enlarged gradually, or dilated. Smaller planes can then be placed within larger planes concentrically, or with slight variations in the direction or position of elements (figs. 145, 146). Alternate positive and negative shapes might be overlapped (fig. 147).

146

145

147

Planar shapes (or flat forms) can be rotated gradually to achieve transformation. The transformed shapes can then be superimposed (fig. 148). In addition, the size of shapes can be altered to suggest receding and advancing elements in space (fig. 149).

As with size variations, alternate positive and negative shapes might be overlapped (fig. 150).

149

148

150

Folding Planes   **Establishing Volume**

A plane can be manipulated to form a round or pointed corner where it is made to fold. Folding might expose the reverse side of a shape, which can then be visualized in outline (figs. 151, 152). A negative line can indicate a sharp fold (fig. 153).

A shape can be thickened along one or more of its edges to establish volume. The combination of lines and planes helps to distinguish the frontal plane from the side planes in a shape (figs. 154, 155).

Volume can be presented with the frontal plane turned obliquely or laterally (figs. 156, 157).

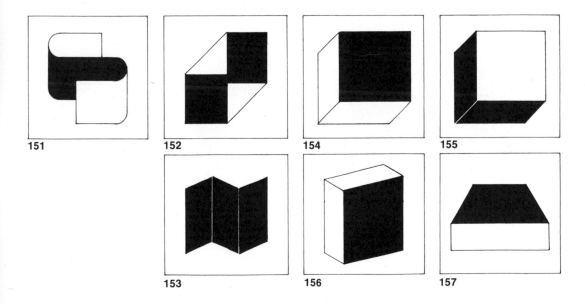

151

152

154

155

153

156

157

Most geometric shapes are regular, or have components with consistent or orderly positions and directions. Shapes should be positioned at predetermined distances (fig. 158). The direction of shapes should be at predetermined angles, establishing fan, circular, or spiral patterns (fig. 159).

With two or four components, a shape might resemble a square (fig. 160). With three components, a triangular shape might result (fig. 161).

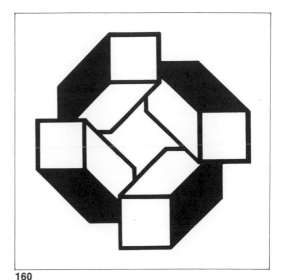

160

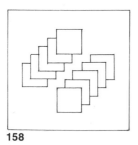

158

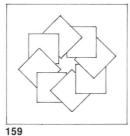

159

161

Deviation

Symmetry

Sometimes strict regularity produces a rigid composition, and some deviation is desirable. Deviation is effectively applied when one or more components change shape, size, position, or direction without seriously disrupting the original design (figs. 162–65).

Symmetrical shapes are regular shapes whose left and right halves are mirror images. An invisible straight line, an *axis,* divides the shape equally (fig. 166). A symmetrical shape can be positioned horizontally or on a slant (fig. 167).

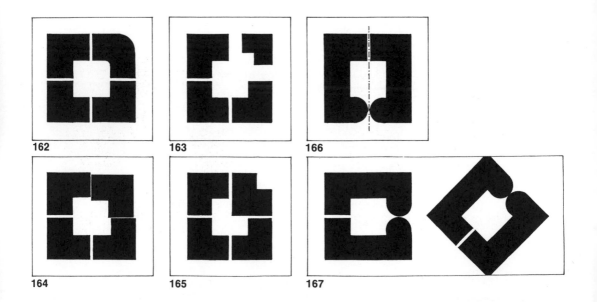

162

163

166

164

165

167

Asymmetry

Slight deviation can be introduced in a symmetrical shape by shifting the two halves out of alignment, by overlapping the halves, or by adding some variation to one of the halves (figs. 168–70).

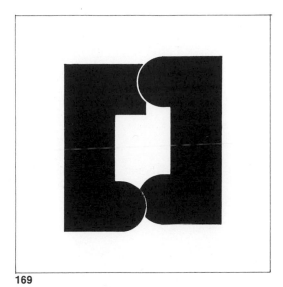

169

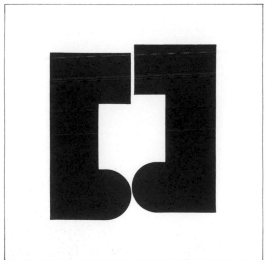

168

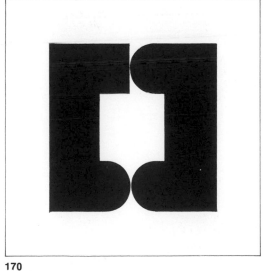

170

Organic shapes are formed of smoothly flowing curves with imperceptible transitions or projecting connections. The curves are usually hand drawn, but drawing instruments, such as French curves or flexible curves, are sometimes used. Straight lines are rarely present. A shape created with curves and straight lines exhibits geometric as well as organic characteristics.

Although simplicity is generally desirable, an organic shape can display intricate details.

A line that flexes in a single direction results in a *C curve* (fig. 171). The other type of curve, an *S curve,* is produced when a line is flexed in two directions (fig. 172). The S curve is actually two C curves joined from opposite directions.

Both C and S curves can be presented as small or large loops (figs. 173, 174).

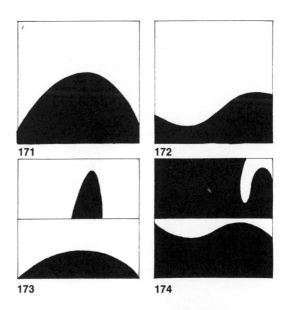

171

172

173

174

Shapes with Pointed Tips

Shapes with Rounded Tips

Two curves that meet can either establish a continuous flow or a pointed tip. Pointed tips can be seen either as projecting from the body of a shape (fig. 175), or as inverted toward it (fig. 177).

Tips that are blunt (figs. 175, 177) can be sharpened by extending the curves near their junction (figs. 176, 178).

Any projecting or inverted tip can be rounded by smoothing the point (figs. 179, 180).

This rounded tip can be exaggerated with a prominent ending (figs. 181, 182).

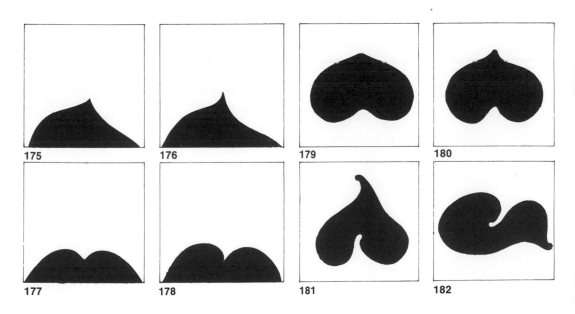

175 176 179 180

177 178 181 182

The Joining and Linking of Shapes

The Splitting, Tearing, and Breaking of Shapes

Two shapes that overlap (fig. 183) can be partially joined (fig. 184).

Two separate shapes (fig. 185) can be linked with protrusions (fig. 186).

A shape (fig. 187) can be split partially or completely into two or more shapes, while the overall image remains intact (figs. 188, 189). The split components might be manipulated to introduce slight variations if desired.

The tearing and breaking of shapes result in ragged edges, which introduce some irregularity (fig. 190).

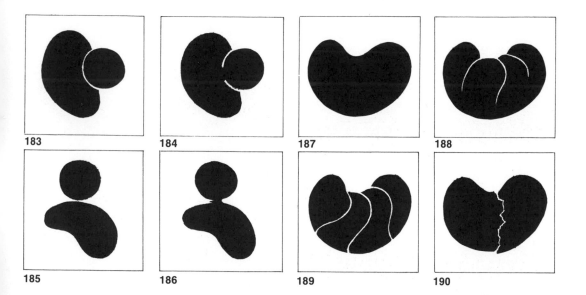

183

184

187

188

185

186

189

190

Cutting and Removing Parts of Shapes

The Curling and Twisting of Shapes

A portion, or portions, of a shape can be cut and removed, altering its edge (fig. 191), or producing negative shapes (figs. 192, 193). Cut edges might be left ragged to suggest a forced break (fig. 194).

A shape can be treated as a soft plane that curls to reveal the bottom or back of the shape (fig. 195).

A shape can also be distorted by twisting it and narrowing its middle (fig. 196).

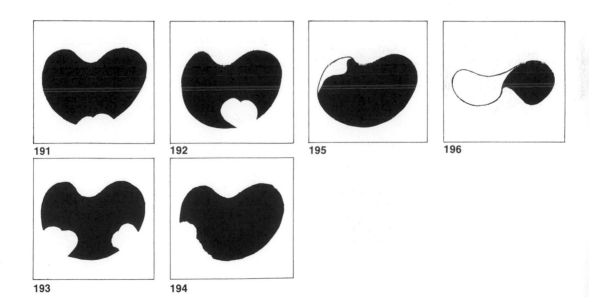

191

192

195

196

193

194

The Rippling and Creasing of Shapes

The Inflation and Deflation of Shapes

The excessive curling of a shape leads to ripples (fig. 197).

Creases created by curling and rippling a shape can be given sharp edges (fig. 198). Creasing can be effected only halfway down the shape (fig. 199).

A shape can be inflated to considerable fullness (approaching a circle) without an obvious increase in size (fig. 200). It can also be deflated, or contracted, becoming crinkled, without an obvious decrease in size (figs. 201, 202).

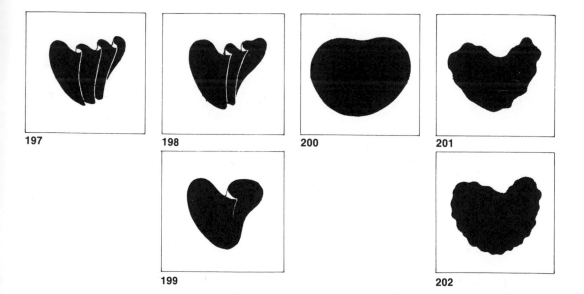

197

198

200

201

199

202

40

The Metamorphosis and Deformation of Shapes

The Proliferation of Shapes

A shape can *metamorphose*—be affected by internal growth in one or more specific areas (fig. 203). It can be *deformed* as if it is being acted upon by some external force that is squeezing, pulling, or pushing it (figs. 204–6).

Multiple use of a shape is called *proliferation* (fig. 207). The size and shape of overlapped or superimposed, proliferated elements can vary (figs. 208–10).

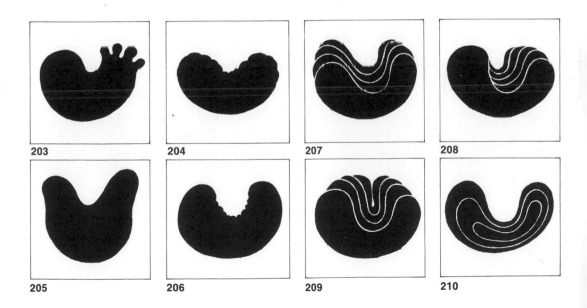

203

204

207

208

205

206

209

210

Symmetrical Expression

Symmetry can be introduced in an organic shape. To achieve strict symmetry, a mirror image can be created of components on either side of an invisible axis (fig. 211). The axis, however, can become a C- or S-shaped curve, and the components can be appropriately adjusted for a symmetrical expression (fig. 212).

Further manipulations of the resultant shape can also be introduced (fig. 213). Components can vary slightly without destroying the symmetry of the structure (fig. 214).

212

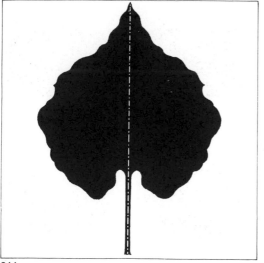

211

213

214

A form, whether abstract or representational, geometric or organic, can be developed into different configurations. The designer can thus examine all possible variations before deciding on one.

Illustrations on the next few pages feature a variety of L-shaped forms (fig. 215).

One way to change the shape of a form is to change the internal area from a solid plane (fig. 215) to an empty space. The form might have a fine or a bold outline (figs. 216, 217).

The form can be split into two or more stripes (fig. 218), covered with a texture or pattern (fig. 219), layered (fig. 220), or given other details (fig. 221).

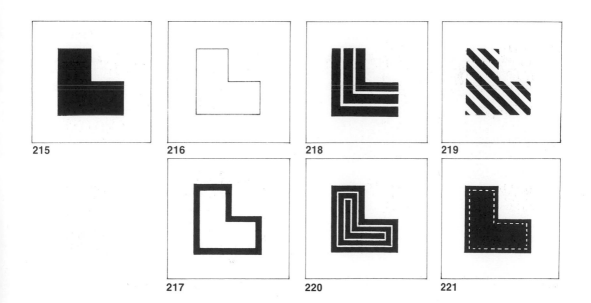

215

216

218

219

217

220

221

External Variation

Extension

The two basic ways to vary a form externally are with corner (fig. 222) and edge variations (fig. 223).

Sometimes internal variations lead to external variations, or vice versa. The combined external-internal variations can establish interesting results (figs. 224, 225).

A form can be extended with a border or concentric layers (fig. 226). Creating a frame of a certain shape (fig. 227), adding a shape to serve as background (fig. 228), or introducing subsequent layers (fig. 229) can also be used as extensions.

222

223

226

227

224

225

228

229

Superimposition

Other forms can be superimposed on a given form without obliterating its general shape (figs. 230–32).

Transfiguration

A form can be *transfigured* by changing a portion of the form or the entire form to something representational (figs. 233–35).

230

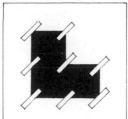

231

233

234

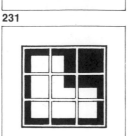

232

235

Dislocation

Distortion

A form can be dissected or broken into two or more parts and then dislocated (figs. 236–38).

The simplest way to distort a form is to change the proportion of its height and width. This can be done by using a superimposed square grid as a guide (fig. 239). A grid of decreased height or narrower width is then drawn to map out a distorted shape (fig. 240).

Diagonal distortion, circular distortion, or any other distortion can be effected in a similar manner (figs. 241, 242).

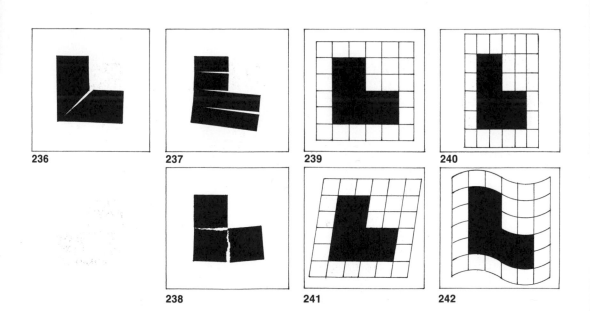

236

237

239

240

238

241

242

A form can be regarded as a three-dimensional plane that might bend, fold, or be seen from different angles and distances (figs. 243–46).

When thickness is added to a form, it acquires volume (fig. 247). It can be rotated in space, displaying a different shape (fig. 248). It can also be made to appear transparent (fig. 249).

An extension to a form can approximate shadows or reflections cast on water (figs. 250–52).

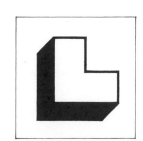

247

248

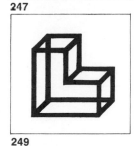

249

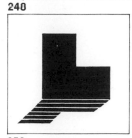

250

243

244

251

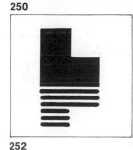

252

245

246

Further Developments

All the previously mentioned methods of developing a form can be combined, producing many more possible configurations (figs. 253–58).

257

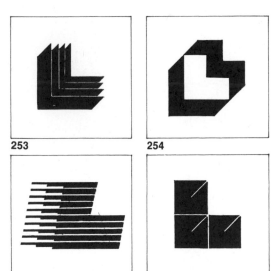

253

254

255

256

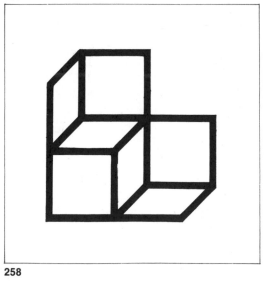

258

PART III
REPRESENTATIONAL FORMS

Most representational forms capture the basic characteristics of shapes and avoid subjects with unusual, less familiar details. For instance, a leaf can be depicted as a shape representing leaves of most deciduous trees, or it can be depicted as a shape representing one particular tree. It is rare, however, that a leaf of an unusual shape is chosen as the subject for a design.

Various ways of designing a form have been suggested in Part II, and these can be applied to the design of representational forms. It should first be decided whether to present a form as a geometric shape or as an organic shape, and how abstract it could be and still satisfy design goals. A preliminary search into a range of specimens is often desirable, so that their particularities can be compared and general features extracted. Drawing a selected specimen or two is necessary for achieving a thorough understanding of the subject.

Natural forms are diverse, but possess the same basic structural characteristics determined by natural laws governing their growth. It is helpful to observe and identify the environmental forces that affect the shapes of natural forms. The shapes of the components of natural forms and how they work together structurally should then be examined.

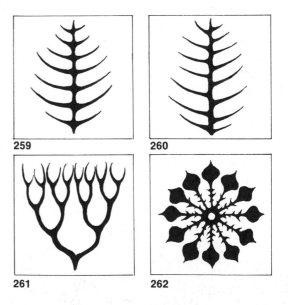

259

260

261

262

Branching and Fanning

Spirals and Undulations

A common feature in the structures of plants and animals is the existence of a backbone or central columnar shape with elements that *branch* bilaterally (fig. 259) or in an alternating pattern (fig. 260). Branching can also take the form of a splitting—one element splits into two, two into four, and so on (fig. 261).

When more than two elements branch, a *fanning* pattern can result. Fanning can extend 360 degrees, with rotating elements emerging from one central point (fig. 262), or surrounding a large open center (fig. 263).

Linear shapes in nature are seldom linear in the geometric sense. These natural shapes actually curl slightly or prominently in one or more directions.

If a linear shape proceeds as a C curve, winding around a center in graduated swirls, a *spiral* is formed (fig. 264). Suggesting three dimensions, a conical (fig. 265) or tubular shape can be created (fig. 266).

If it proceeds as an S curve, narrow or wide *undulations* result (figs. 267, 268). Undulations can form a grooved shape or chain to suggest a third dimension (figs. 269, 270).

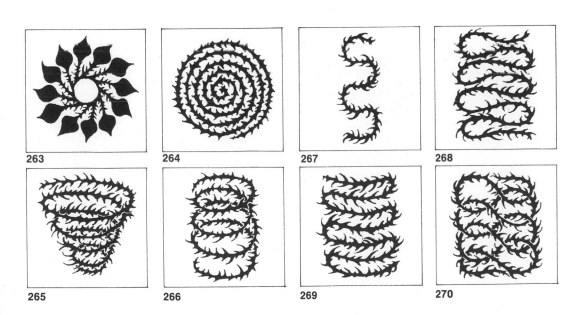

263

264

267

268

265

266

269

270

Elements within a particular natural form —cells, sections, or layers that make up a surface—usually display *affinity* (figs. 271, 272). These elements are not strict repetitions, but vary individually or progressively to conform to an overall shape and structure. There might be several types of elements, with affinity among elements of the different types.

Affinity establishes *unity*. Unity is also established by fitting elements tightly together (fig. 273). Transitions create a smooth flow between elements (fig. 274).

Man-made forms are either crafted with tools by hand or manufactured with machines. Generally, tools and machines are efficient at creating straight lines, flat surfaces, right angles, circles, and cylinders. This explains why most man-made forms display a geometric configuration. Organic shapes are sometimes introduced as decorations, or for ergonomic reasons.

The nature of its materials and the assembly of its parts are important considerations when observing a man-made form. It is also important to study the form from different viewpoints.

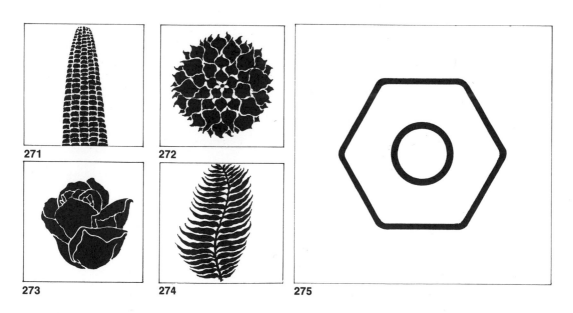

271

272

273

274

275

52

Materials can be thin sheets or solid masses, soft or hard, transparent or opaque, light or heavy. Materials used to fabricate man-made forms can be singular or can be parts that are assembled.

Parts can be assembled by fitting them, bonding them, or joining them with springs, pivots, or hinges, which allow for movement.

Man-made forms are often conceived as *plans* and *elevations.* Viewing the form from above establishes its plan (fig. 275). Viewing it from the front and sides establishes its elevations (figs. 276, 277). Plan and elevation studies are the basic ways of visualizing a man-made form.

The form is then studied from different viewpoints, or *perspectives* (fig. 278). It must be noted that most planes are distorted when seen in perspective.

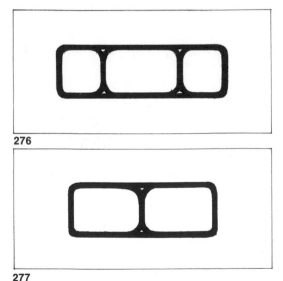

276

277

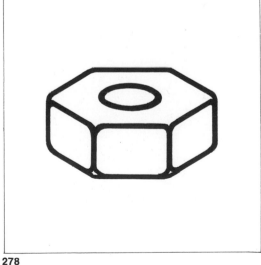

278

53

Designing with representational forms can begin with a series of self-contained compositions—singular forms, plural forms, and/or compound forms that are established without a frame of reference. These might then be contained within specific frames of reference to help define spatial relationships.

To create a *singular form,* the chosen subject is first studied from different viewpoints with drawings and sketches. One drawing (fig. 279) is then selected and used as the basis for design development. Consideration is given to aspects of aesthetics as well as communication. The singular form can be visualized as one solid plane (fig. 280), planes displaying details (fig. 281), lines (fig. 283), the combination of lines and planes (figs. 282, 284, 285), or a textured shape (fig. 286).

279

280

281

282

283

284

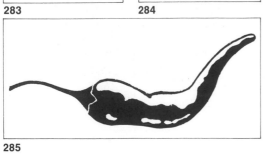

285

286

Repeating a singular form establishes a *plural form* (fig. 287). The singular forms, now components, could vary externally and/or internally (fig. 288). They could touch, overlap, join, or remain separate. Joining representational forms can result in a rather unnaturalistic, yet interesting design (fig. 289). Separate forms must be adjacent, with one intruding the semienclosed space of the other if they are to be considered plural (fig. 290).

Two or more components can be arranged in accordance with the following concepts:

a. *translation*—varying the positions, but not the directions, of components (fig. 291)

b. *rotation*—varying the directions, with minimal change in position, of components (figs. 292–95)

c. *reflection*—creating components as mirror images (figs. 296–98)

d. *dilation*—increasing the size of superimposed or adjacent components (fig. 299)

Positions of components are also effected with rotation and reflection and frequently with dilation. Positional changes in such cases should be kept to a minimum.

Components can also be grouped randomly, or using a combination of the concepts described above (figs. 300–306).

287

288

56

289

290

291

292

57

293

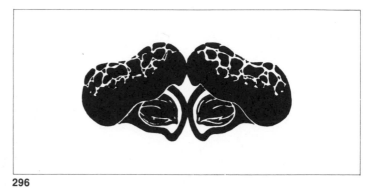

296

294

297

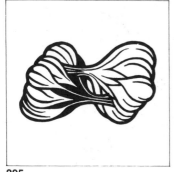

295

298

299

300

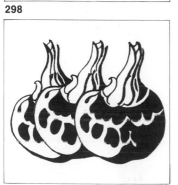

301

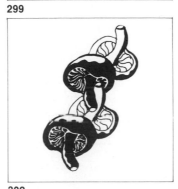

302

303

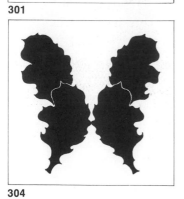

304

305

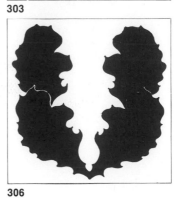

306

A compound form is established with dissimilar components, or with similar *and* dissimilar components. Used in a self-contained composition, a compound form can be taken as a singular form (figs. 307–9).

Plural forms can be based on compound forms, producing more intricate designs (figs. 310–14).

307

308

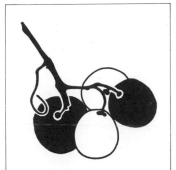

309

310

311

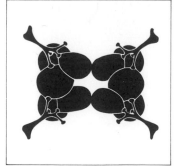

312

313

314

Singular, plural, or compound forms can be applied as unit or superunit forms in repetition within a definite frame of reference. Their regular arrangement could establish a *formal* composition—all elements are organized in a kind of mathematical order.

Repetition involves reproducing the same shape in a design as well as placing the shapes at intervals, which can be determined with lines forming an invisible structural grid.

The simplest composition with repetition involves the arrangement of unit or superunit forms as two-way continuance, resulting in *rows* that can extend vertically, horizontally, or at any given angle (figs. 315, 316).

The row does not have to be straight. It can be crooked or curved. Unit forms can display a change of direction regularly within the row if desired.

315

316

Four-way Continuance

When rows of unit or superunit forms are repeated regularly, four-way continuance is achieved (fig. 317).

Compositions with four-way continuance create a patternlike design (figs. 318–27). If a space is not completely filled, the composition becomes less formal (figs. 328, 329).

318

317

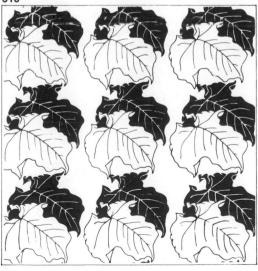

319

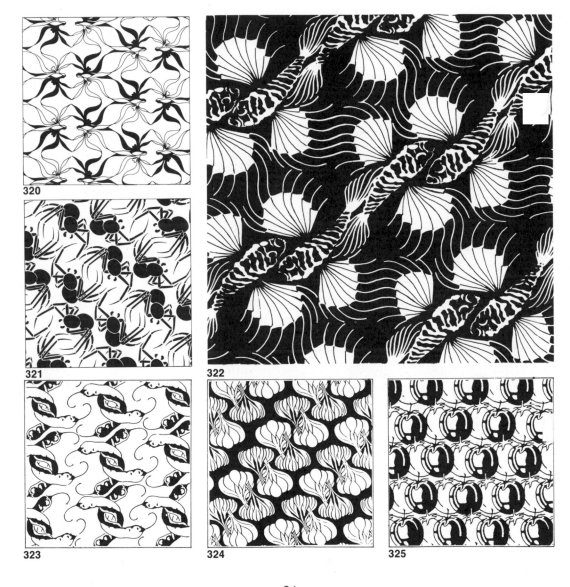

320

321

322

323

324

325

326

327

328

329

A structural grid can comprise triangles
to guide the placement of unit forms.
This produces a six-way continuance,
with shapes grouped as triangles or hex-
agons. If each unit form consists of a
head and a tail, it is interesting to
observe that the heads will meet at one
point and the tails will meet at another
point, in an alternating manner (figs.
330–34).

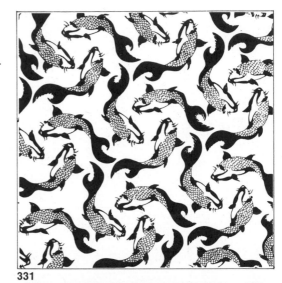

331

330

332

Development and Variations of the Repetition Structure

333

Unit forms can be photocopied (or traced) and cut out to explore all possible repetitions. A form can also be traced and then flipped over to obtain a mirror image (fig. 335). Superunit forms created this way can relate to each other in a different pattern of repetition, resulting in regular, but not monotonous, compositions (figs. 336–41). Isolated background shapes can be changed from white to black to achieve variations (figs. 342–44).

The structural grid can can be made visible as actual lines of definite breadth, or made to become edges of spatial cells, embellishing the unit or superunit forms (figs. 345–47).

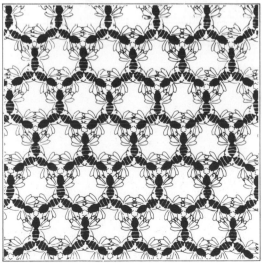

334

335

336

337

338

339

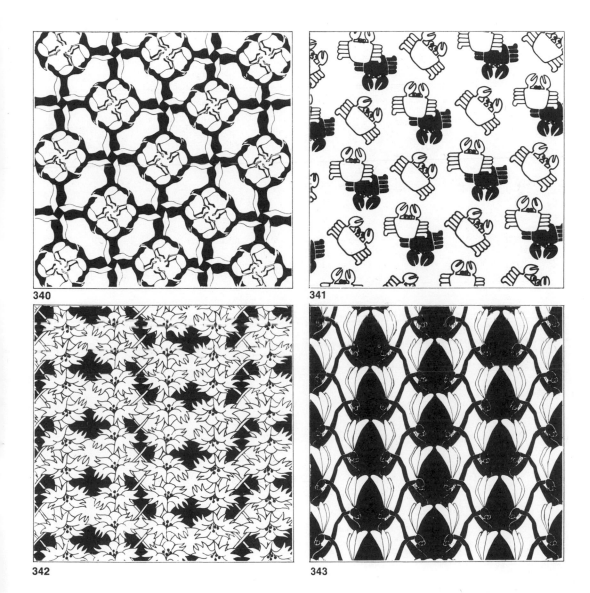

340

341

342

343

344

345

346

347

The repetition of unit or superunit forms around a common center results in *radiation,* which is a technique used in formal compositions.

The basic structural grid for a design with radiation has a *center of reference* —the meeting point of all radiating lines, or the point around which structural lines revolve. Radiation normally features lines that converge near the center, with space between lines increasing as they move away from the center.

Structural lines guide the placement of unit or superunit forms that are directly linked to or equidistant from the center of reference.

The 360-degree rotation of unit or superunit forms results in full radiation. The center of reference could be the point at which lines converge, either exactly, overlapping, or at some regular distance from the center of reference. The angle of rotation for each form must be consistent to establish regularity (fig. 348).

Rotating forms less than 360 degrees results in segmentary radiation (fig. 349). The fan or arc effect that results admits considerable background space near the center of radiation.

348

349

A superunit form composed of translated unit forms can be rotated to achieve radiation (fig. 350).

Rotated unit forms displaying radiation can be used as a superunit form for translation in a repetition structure (figs. 351, 352).

351

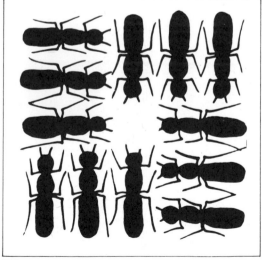

350

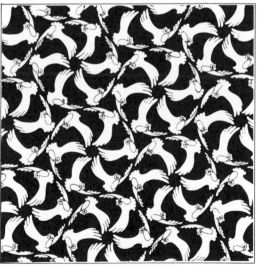

352

Rotation and Reflection

Rotation and Dilation

A full radiation might be cropped and joined to its mirror image on the other side of the cropped edge, which functions as an axis for reflection (fig. 353).

Dilated forms can be used instead of forms of uniform size. Slight variations of shape can be introduced during dilation if desired. These forms can be rotated to achieve a segmentary radiation, and then reflected or rotated again to achieve full radiation (figs. 354, 355).

Dilated forms in rotation can result in a spiral arrangement, a kind of radiation (fig. 356).

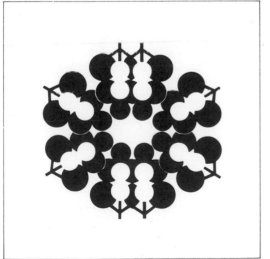

353

354

355

After establishing radiation, a composition could be superimposed with structural lines, making parallel or concentric subdivisions that intercept the forms. The interception could result in the dissection and partial dislocation of forms (figs. 357–61).

356

357

358

359

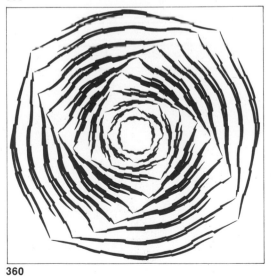

360

361

Gradation refers to the systematic altera-tion of the shape, size, position, direc-tion, or proportion of a form. The forms produced by these changes are then arranged in sequence, with smooth tran-sitions between forms.

Unit forms in gradation can be posi-tioned according to a regular repetition structure with gradual variations. Unit forms can also be positioned with increasing or decreasing density.

Gradation of shape can be achieved by varying a form internally and/or exter-nally.

External without internal variation is achieved by adding to or subtracting from the form (fig. 362). Creating inter-nal without external variations requires more prominent gradations. In most cases, shape gradations affect the exter-nal and internal aspects of a form (fig. 363). Any form can be changed to any other form with the appropriate number of shape gradations.

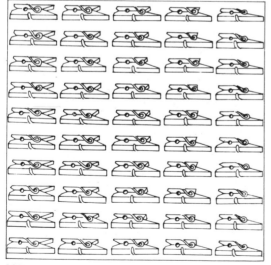

362

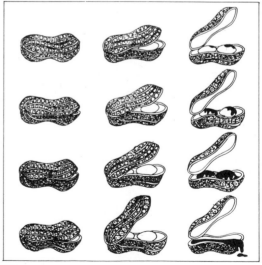

363

Gradation of Size

Gradation of Position

Size can be altered by enlarging or reducing forms arranged in sequence (usually in repetition). The transition could move from light to heavy rhythms, from heavy to light, or in an alternating fashion (fig. 364).

This is possible in a repetition structure with active structural lines that intercept and partially crop forms. The height of forms decreases as they are gradually moved down along the structural line (fig. 365).

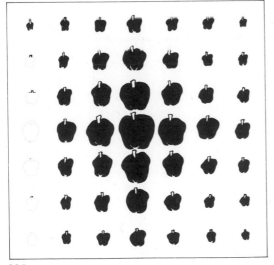

364

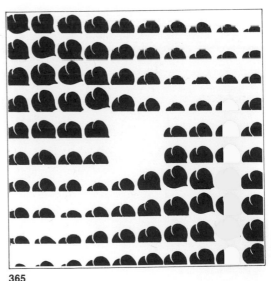

365

Gradation of Direction

Rotating a form from left to right on a flat surface, while maintaining its shape, effects a change in direction (figs. 366, 367). It can also change direction if it is rotated from front to back in three-dimensional space; different views are seen as different shapes (figs. 368, 369).

Figure 370 features directional changes from left to right and from front to back, as well as gradations of shape and size.

367

366

368

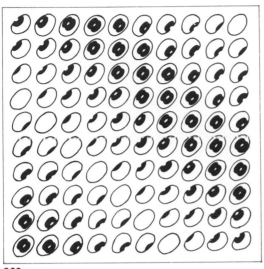

369

The narrowing and widening of subdivisions in a gradation structure might demand the narrowing and widening of forms. Forms altered this way are affected by gradation of proportion, which involves considerable shape distortions (figs. 371–73).

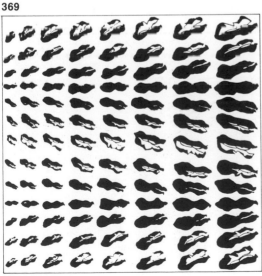

370

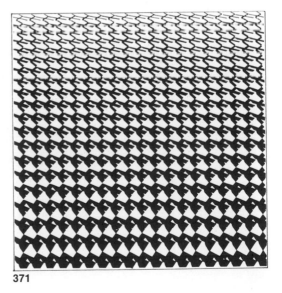

371

79

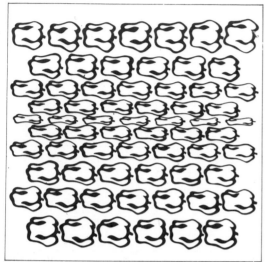

372

If the shape, size, color, or texture of unit forms in a composition varies slightly, they are not part of a strict repetition, but are more loosely, or *similarly,* related.

Similarity can also describe the placement of unit forms; the similar arrangement of unit forms might resemble a repetition, radiation, or a gradation structure.

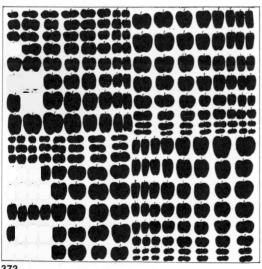

373

374

80

375

376

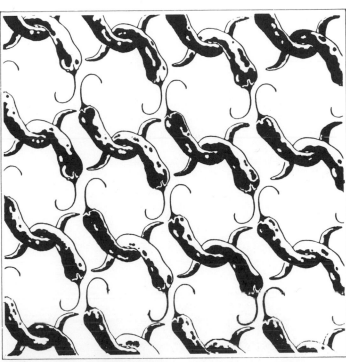

378

377

379

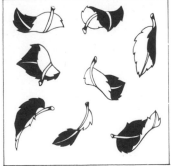

380

Similarity and Repetition

Similarity and Radiation

The visual effect of close similarity is much like that of repetition. Similarity is achieved when a form is repeated with slight external and/or internal variations (figs. 374, 375). Forms in nature are never strict repetitions; no two leaves on the same tree are identical.

Similarity can also be established by rotating a form and displaying different views (fig. 376).

A formal structure can comprise similarly related forms that are not arranged in any sequence, introducing an element of informality to the design (figs. 377–79).

A more informal design is achieved when the similarly related forms are distributed with similar density (fig. 380).

Rotated similar forms on a flat surface can be grouped regularly or freely to suggest radiation (figs. 381, 382).

381

382

COMPOSITIONS WITH CONCENTRATION

The arrangement of unit forms can proceed from dense to sparse in moderately smooth transitions to suggest gradation (fig. 383).

Figure 384 illustrates this effect, but also features superimposed structural lines that intercept and crop the unit forms.

Concentration is the gathering of unit forms in particular areas of a composition. This establishes rhythmic movements, often creating a center of interest and subordinate accents.

Concentration can be associated with natural phenomena—fleeting clouds, splashing water, falling leaves, migrating birds.

383

384

Points of Concentration

A point in a composition can mark the densest concentration of unit forms. Density could gradually give way to the sparse placement of elements; loose elements could activate otherwise blank space (figs. 385, 386).

When there is more than one point of concentration, densities at the different points should vary, allowing one point to emerge as the center of interest. In dense areas, voids become prominent; a void is often the center of interest in a composition with tightly packed elements (fig. 387).

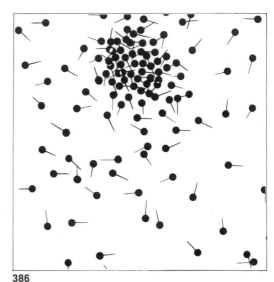

386

385

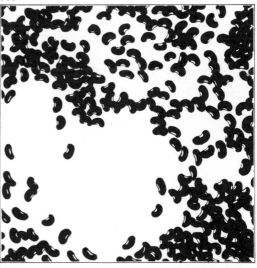

387

Linear Concentration

A concentrated area in a design can be linear, forming a band, with or without loose elements nearby (figs. 388–90).

Unit forms within the band could vary in density (fig. 391). A composition could contain more than one band (fig. 392).

389

388

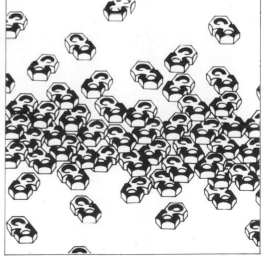
390

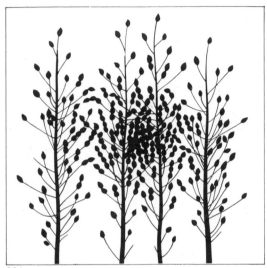

Unit forms can be brought together as a plane of almost even density. The plane could be an isolated shape within the frame of reference or could partially extend beyond it (fig. 393).

391

392

393

Contrast is used to suggest visual distinctions. Increased contrast enhances visibility. Decreased contrast assimilates elements in a composition. In most cases, contrast is used intuitively by the designer, but it can be consciously applied to effect comparisons and to establish a center of interest.

Contrast can refer to the appearance, placement, or quantity of forms.

Contrast can be applied to one or more aspects of a form's appearance—its shape, size, color or texture.

Contrasting shapes can differ externally or internally, or have different basic shapes (figs. 394, 395). Contrast can be introduced by relating large and small forms (figs. 396–99).

In a black-and-white design, a planar form and a linear form establish contrasting tones (figs. 400–402). Contrast of texture happens when some forms display fine details and others are plainly visualized forms (figs. 403–5).

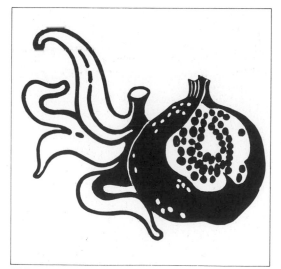

394

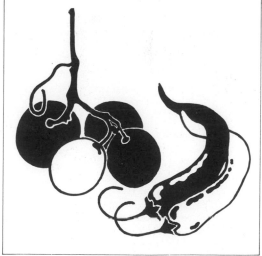

395

396

397

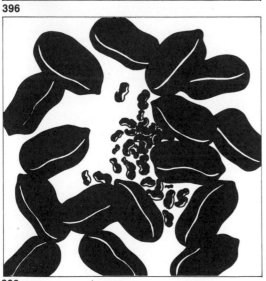

398

399

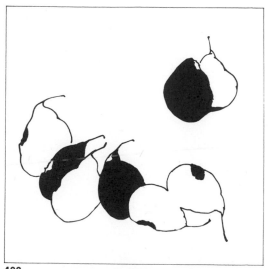

400

401

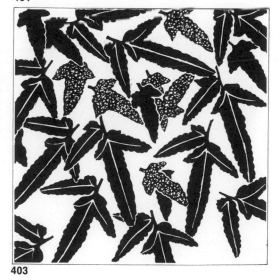

402

403

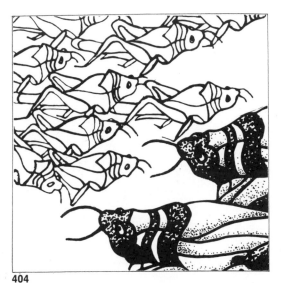

404

Contrast of placement refers to the position, direction, and spatial relationships of forms.

Contrast of position refers to the arrangement of forms within the frame of reference (figs. 406, 407).

Forms arranged in conflicting directions establish contrast (figs. 408, 409). Contrast of direction can also be achieved by rotating forms and presenting different views (fig. 410).

Overlapping forms suggest depth (fig. 411). Forms of varying sizes suggest relative distances (fig. 412).

405

406

90

407

408

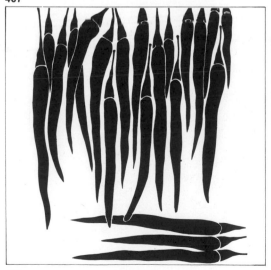

409

410

411

Contrast of quantity refers to the density and sparseness of elements in a composition when only one type of unit form is used (fig. 413).

Contrast of quantity as mass and void can be arranged as forms surrounding a blank area, or as forms gathered closely with a surrounding void (figs. 414, 415).

If two types of unit forms are used, fewer instances of one form can be contrasted with many instances of another (figs. 416–19).

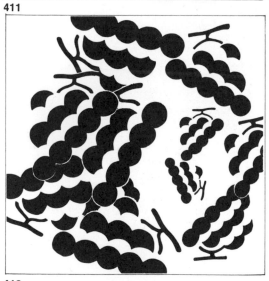

412

413

414

415

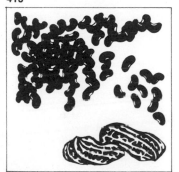

416

417

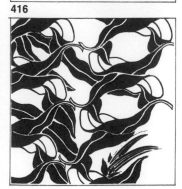

419

418

The combination of regular and irregular elements in a design establishes *anomaly*. Because regular elements are more numerous than irregular ones, anomaly also features contrasting quantities.

Anomaly can be introduced only in formal compositions with a repetition, radiation, or a gradation structure. The strict regularity of the composition makes a slight irregularity prominent.

Anomaly can be effected with the variation of shape, size, color, texture, position, or direction. An anomalous element usually marks the center of interest. Several anomalous elements can acccentuate different aspects of the design. Anomalous elements introduced too frequently lose their distinction as such and are seen as another set of unit forms.

The presence of a form different in shape from the unit forms introduces an anomaly. The shape can be completely different, or have only external and/or internal variations (figs. 420–22).

420

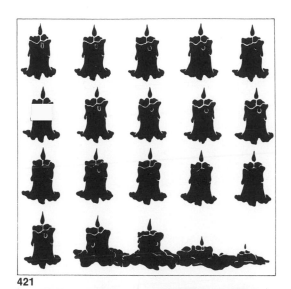

A particularly large or small form among unit forms of the same size introduces another type of anomaly. Fitting a large form into the composition might require the removal of some smaller unit forms (fig. 423).

421

422

423

Anomaly in Color

Anomaly in Texture

One unit form can be changed from a planar shape to a linear shape to introduce anomaly in "color" to a black-and-white design (fig. 424).

When one or more unit forms display texture or more details, anomaly in texture results (fig. 425).

424

425

Anomaly in Position and Direction

One or more unit forms can be dislocated in a composition, achieving anomaly in position and/or direction (figs.
426–28).

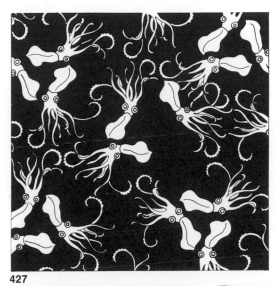

427

426

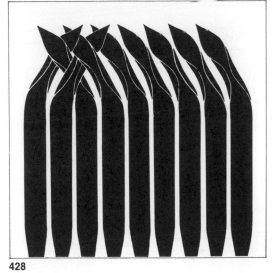

428

INDEX